Uniquely
Created

Uniquely Created

I am God's Masterpiece
(Ephesians 2:10)

DONNA E. WARREN

ISBN 978-1-957582-97-9 (paperback)
ISBN 978-1-957582-96-2 (eBook)

Printed in the United States of America

Contents

Acknowledgments

Biblical quotes are from KJV (King James Version) of the Holy Bible, unless otherwise noted.

The author of any quotes is listed by the quote unless unknown.

Thanks to my family and friends for their continued support and encouragement. Special thanks to my brother, Rev. James Butler, Jr. for his "About the Author".

I continue to give full honor, glory and praise to my Lord and Savior, Jesus, the Christ, for the comfort, strength and talents He has given me.

Dedication

This book is dedicated to the men and women who give of their time and talents, every day, to help make this a better and safer place.

May you continue to Go, Do, and Be all that God has called you to be.

About the Author....

Yet, O Lord, you are our Father.
We are the clay, you are the potter,
We arc the work of your hands.
(Isaiah 64:8)

It is ever amazing the stations in life in which we find ourselves. A more accurate statement is, it is amazing the stations in life that find us. This collection speaks to the various stations or occupations that our Creator, the Potter, has molded us to fill. When we find ourselves in them, it is a perfect fit, perfectly shaped for the gifts and graces given us.

The Author is one who has found herself in her God ordained place. Donna E. Warren, the oldest of eight children, was raised on and is a co-owner of a Tennessee Century Farm in Murfreesboro, TN. Donna (Elaine) has been married to John H. Warren for over 50 years. The Warrens reside in Mansfield, Texas. They have two daughters and three grandchildren.

Elaine has a Bachelor's degree in Elementary Education and a Master's in Elementary Education with an Early Childhood Specialization. She is a Certified Daycare Director and is also certified to write curriculum for children. She is a retired educator with over 36 years of experience. Elaine is passionate about her Christian Faith and can be found being about her Father's business.

Elaine has written six other books of inspirational poetry as well as two children's books. I know that this work will be a great source of inspiration to all, just as my big sister, Elaine, is a great source of inspiration to me.

The Reverend James L. Butler Jr.
(Elaine's only brother and self-proclaimed favorite sibling).

"Sing the wonderous love of Jesus,
sing His mercy
and His grace!
from the song
"When We all Get to Heaven"

By Eliza E. Hewitt
and
Emily D. Wilson

Use Your Stone

"Do not neglect the gift you have...
1 Timothy 4:14

David, a youthful boy
with a sling and a stone in hand –
did bring to Israel peace and joy
when with his hand and faith in God, Goliath slay.
For God provides us all the tools we need to succeed.
I urgently plead,
"Use your stone".
Use your stone to overcome the giants in your life.
You can combat tribulation and strife.
Step forward on faith and your talent-
Make God's stone to you – relevant.
If you can speak – use your words to build up and encourage.
If you can teach – enlighten a mind.
If you can pray – pray for others-giving them a gift of love.

Let not fear, depression, conformity, greed or pain

in your life reign.

Use your stone-

for with God at your side, you are never alone.

David had a sling and a stone.

Joshua, seven days did march.

Moses, a staff did carry.

Abram left home; he did not tarry.

Each used his stone, moved outside their comfort zone

and walked by faith-

"God, who gives peace (was) with (them). Phil. 4:9 CEV

Use your stone.

You are never alone.

Modern Day Nightingales

"We who are strong (in faith) have an obligation to bear
With the failings of the weak, and not to please ourselves.
Romans 15:1 (ESV)

Nursing is a noble, yet challenging profession

For the well-being of the patient depends
greatly upon a nurse's connection.

For nurses are UNIQUELY prepared for the challenges they
encounter, daily, by using kindness, patience and compassion.

These qualities enable the patient to relax and develop a sense
of trust which enable them, in their health, to participate.

This may help them get discharged at an earlier date.

God gives us gifts to use and share, but nurses
are called to serve of His grace.

Grace that enables them to utilize the gifts they have been given to encourage, retain knowledge, listen, have patience and compassion to those entrusted whose health they embrace.

"God said, Let us make man in our image, after our likeness," and felt "man" needed a special kind of person to take care of them, thus gave them "grace" in the form of a nurse.

Nurses see patients as being worthy of love and care.

Thus, they go the extra mile, their love, to share.

"Love never ends", 1 Cor. 13:8a.

Many waters cannot quench love; rivers cannot wash it away. Song of Solomon 8:7

Nurses serve to their fullest capacity willingly.

Therefore, we applaud them with sincerity.

Nurse's Prayer

Dear Lord, let me receive the sick
And traumatized with an open and giving heart.
Give to my efforts success so that life may
continue, if it be your will. Without you
I cannot succeed.
Let me have no purpose except the
glorification of life.
Grant that the sick that you have
placed in my care be abundantly blessed,
and not one of them be lost due to any
neglect on my part.
Help me to overcome any temporal weakness
so that I may my fullest capacity.
Let me always reach out to all in Joy, compassion
and with a loving heart.

By *begood74*

Never Alone

Dr. Mae Jameison once stated, "Never be
limited by other peoples' imaginations. If you
adopt their attitudes, then the possibility won't
exist because you'll already shut it out. You
can hear other peoples' wisdom, but you've
got to re-evaluate the world for yourself."

Children of God-as you continue to realize
Your dreams and ambitions-
To thyself and God-always be true.
Remember Psalm 24:1 KJV – "The earth is the
Lord's and the fullness thereof: and they
that dwell therein."
You are never alone.
Gpd is with you now as He was when your life first begun.
You are never alone.
Matthews 28:20 CEV – "I am with you always,
to the very end of the age."
You are never alone.
Imagination. Preparation. Dedication>
These three things and faith in God
will enable you to achieve the sincere desires of your heart.
You are never alone.

Doctor of Dental Surgery

_____ - a solo Practitioner is he.

Awarded a Doctor of Dental Surgery Degree

for his innate ability

to diagnose, prevent and treat tooth diseases

and provide instruction on diet, brushing and flossing daily.

He meets his patients' needs with agility

as he continues to promote good dental health

for both his patients and family.

1 Cor. 12:9 reads, "To others the Spirit has

given great faith or power

To heal the sick or the power to work mighty miracles."

The Spirit gave _____ diagnostic ability

and manual skills –

skills that he has further improved over the years.

Good communication, business sense, self-discipline,

good visual memory, excellent judgement regarding space and shape-

all a very knowledgeable, skillful and exemplary dentist creates.

Teeth and gums – flossing and brushing -tooth extractions
Cavity filling – plastic sealants
…the list is endless and most revealing.
X-ray machines, drills, mouth mirror, probes, forceps
and other equipment galore.
Masks, gloves and safety glasses protect
from infectious diseases and more.
_____ (along with his staff), a DDS is he,
here to serve both you and me.

June 30, 2005

Teachers... the Heart of Education

The old Indian proverb- "It takes a village (community) to raise a child" is most certainly true –

For we see it being done by those such as you.

You share your knowledge every day.

You find joy and satisfaction in the talent you possess.

Your dedication you readily display.

For it is better to see sermons than hear one, you must confess. Faculty and staff of all schools far and near are doing wonderful things when they help shape the lives of future leaders by taking the children under their wing.

For children are like flowers that might wilt and almost die unless given a little loving and gentle care. Striving as you, your concern and love you share. Once again, they are revived to grow and truly achieve, for once again ,someone, in them, believe.

Ephesians 4:16 states "The effective working by which
every part foes its share, causes growth of the body".

When you have a faithful heart and make every attempt to do
your part - then you have brightened the corner where you are.

We give thanks to God for the love educators share
with children everywhere. To them a dozen roses are
given for the godly example they try to be.

It takes a village…is most certainly true. Our schools
are special because of educators such as you.

Retired Educators – Never

"The Spirit has given us a special way to serve others.
Some of us can speak with wisdom, while others
Can speak with knowledge,
but these gifts came from the same Spirit.
1 Cor. 12:7-8 (CEV)

***

The term "retired educator" is, indeed, an oxymoron.
"True" educators, whether retired or not,
continue to answer the call of anyone who
ask because they know that learning is always meaningful.
**One of the most important roles of an educator
is to encourage.**

Educators never really retire,
But continue to safeguard the future well-being of all generations
as they use their God-given gifts to continually inspire.
**One of the most important roles of an educator
is to encourage.**

Armed with perseverance and the patience God gave Job,
they continue to teach, enlighten, train and cultivate –
thus, giving the child something positive to imitate.
**One of the most important roles of an educator
is to encourage.**

With love and determination, an educator (retired or not)
inspires a child by giving them knowledge.
Knowledge which prepares them for their future –
which continues way beyond the life of college.
**One of the most important roles of an educator
is to encourage.**

A "retired educator" – NEVER!
They know that "T teach is to touch a life forever".
**For one of the most important roles of an educator
is to encourage.**

School Counselors

"The purpose in a man's heart is like deep water,
but a man of understanding will draw it out.
Proverbs 20:5 NIV

School Counselors serve a variety of different functions,
for with each child, she cannot make the same assumption.
The assistance counselors provide for students, not only help
them to stay happy and healthy throughout their education.
It assures that in their full academic potential
they believe, receive and achieve.
Emotional and social issues, vocational guidance, mediation
and early intervention is the role they hold every day.
Communication, friendliness, strength and empathy
is what a child needs, not sympathy.
Proverbs 15:22 reads "Without counsel plans fail,
but with many advisers they succeed."
The work and dedication, of school counselors, to our students
is the gift that keeps on giving.
Reach out and thank your school counselor today,
for they work hard to aid a child in the art of living.

February 7, 2022

Life Lessons

THE GIRL SCOUT PROMISE:

*On my honor, I will try: To serve God and my Country,
to help people at all times, and to live by the Girl Scout Law.*

These words, spoken with 3 fingers of her right raised and
the thumb holding down the pinky, gave new meaning to
the path _____ would as she developed into a young
woman with leadership qualities and ethical character.

The Girl Scout Promise would always be on her
heart as she served both man and God.

For God, II Timothy 4:2, has asked that one should preach
the word, be instant in season, out of season, reprove,
rebuke, exhort with long-suffering and doctrine.

In other words, one must be ready, on their honor, to lead
by example and remain steadfast in what is right.

_____ has remained focused and disciplined.

She preserved, maintained a belief in both herself
and God. Thus, in her ultimate success.

On May 28, 2021, _____ saw the results of her labor as she crossed from Junior to Cadette.

She achieved because she believed.

All are to be commended for their dedication to this young lady for the Life Lessons she has learned:

Honesty, friendliness, helpfulness, being caring, courageous and strong, responsible, respectful and resourceful.

_____, you are all that and more.

Congratulations! *(2021)*

I Am Prepared

THE SCOUT OATH:

On my honor, I will do my best
to do my duty to God and my country and to obey the Scout Law:
To help other people at all times, to keep myself physically strong,
mentally awake and morally straight.
These words spoken with his right hand raised in the Scout sign
Gave new meaning to the path _____ would follow
as he developed into a young man with leadership
qualities and ethical character.
The Scout motto: "Be Prepared" would always be on his heart
as he served both God and man.
God, in Timothy 4:2 has asked that one should
"Preach the word, be instant in season, out of season;
reprove, rebuke, exhort with longsuffering and doctrine.
In other words, one must always "be prepared"
to lead by example and remain steadfast in what is right.
_____ remained focused and disciplined.
He preserved, maintained a belief in both himself
and God to reach his ultimate success.

Today, July 31st, 2005, _____ sees the results of his labor
as the highest rank a scout can achieve "Eagle Scout" is awarded.
He achieved because he believed.
Parents and Scout Leaders, you are to be commended
for your dedication to this young man.
Not only for the 21 merit badges (for Eagle Scout) he has earned,
but also, for the Life Lessons he has learned.
Trustworthy, loyal, friendly, obedient,
kind, thrifty, brave, helpful, courteous, clean, cheerful and reverent.
_____, you are all that and more.

Congratulations!!
2005

Motivational Quotes

"Don't worry about failures,
worry about the chances you miss when you don't even try."
Jack Canfield

"It is never too late to be what you might have been."
George Eliot

"Do not let what you cannot do interfere
with what you can do."
John Wooden

"An obstacle is often a steppingstone."
Prescott

If you don't risk anything, you risk even more."
Erica Jong

"Believe you can and you're halfway there "
Theodore Roosevelt

"Wherever life plants you, bloom with grace."
French Proverb

On the Threshold

"And he said unto them, "Go ye into all the world,
and preach the gospel to every creature."
Mark 16:15 KJV

Charles Wesley – 81 years his life did span – wrote
the following words with pen in hand:
"A charge to keep I have.
A God to glorify.
A never-dying soul to save
A fit it for the sky."
He helped others to understand the seriousness of Jesus' command.
For to be given a "trust" by the Lord above is an honor,
A privilege and evidence of God's true love.
So, Rev. _____, as you continue your spiritual journey,
To thyself always be true.
Make full use of the gift God has given you.
An ordinary person you may be,
But your extraordinary ability is what God does see.
Fast when you must, yet always pray.
God crafted the road map and has shown you the way.

For when the charge was given – you did not fret,

But with strength and determination,

the trials and tribulations you met.

"A charge to keep" – YOU HAVE!

Also, a God to glorify.

Always a never-dying soul to save

To fit it for Heaven on high." God called.

You answered, "Here am I".

Congratulations!

Donna Warren

May 12, 2004

Go Preach My Gospel

"The he sent them to tell about God's Kingdom and to heal the sick"
Luke 9:2 NIV
"Go preach My Gospel," saith the Lord,
"Bid the whole earth My grace receives.
He shall be saved that rusts My word,
He shall be damned that won't believe.

These words, written by Isaac Watts in1709,
You, Rev. _____, heard and did indeed heed.
You took the initiative and into the world did tread
to bring to all people the word of God.

Your trusted and gifted leadership never faltered and never failed
as you used your God-given gift-
souls to save and spirits to lift.

Because of your perseverance,
Kingdom Community Church was founded
and upon a solid rock was built.

"Go preach my Gospel," saith the Lord".
Those words you took to heart –
Rolled up your sleeves and knelt in pray as you gave your life to God.

Founding Pastor, Rev. _____ -
as you continue your spiritual journey –
to thyself always be true.
Continue to make use of the gifts
our Lord, God, has given to you.

Congratulations on your Appreciation and
Founding Pastor Installation.
"And he said unto them, "Go into all the world
and preach the gospel to all creation".
Mark 16:15 NIV

Donna Warren
March 24, 2006

Uniquely Created

The 11th hour of the 11th day of the 11th month of 1918
Armistice Day was born and was first celebrated in 1919.
It was renamed Veteran's Day in 1938,
and is dedicated to American Veterans (living or dead) of all wars.
1 Cor. 16:13- "Be on your guard; stand firm in faith; be strong".
To the men and women in the military,
we honor you for your sacrifice and
your service.
God uniquely created you, the people we can
count on when times are tough.

U.S. Coast Guard – initially est. 1790 / created Jan. 28, 1915
(Operates as a service of the Navy)
Colors: Orange and Blue
"Semper Paratus"
(Always ready)
We salute you!

U.S. Army – founded June 14, 1775
Colors: Black & Gold
"This we'll defend."
We salute you!

U.S. Navy – founded October 13, 1775
Colors: Blue & Gold
"Valor and Glory"
We salute you!

U.S. Marines – founded November 10, 1775

Colors: Scarlet & Gold

"Semper Fi"

(Always faithful; always loyal)

We salute you!

U.S. Air Force – founded September 18, 1947

Colors: Ultramarine Blue & Gold

"Fly Fight Win"

We salute you!

Psalm 139:9-10 "I rise on wings of the dawn, if I settle
on the far side of the sea, even there your hand will
guide me – your right hand will hold me fast".
We are proud that we are Americans, and we thank
all veterans for your sacrifices and your service.
Most of all, we give thanks to God for you -
The uniquely created men and women of the United Armed Forces.

More Motivational Quotes

"I am thankful for all of those who said NO to me.
It's because of them I'm doing it myself".
Albert Einstein

"Success is the sum of small efforts repeated day in and day out'".
Robert Collier

"Even if you're on the right track, you'll get
run over if you just sit there".
Will Rodgers

"Success seems to be connected with action. Successful people
keep moving. They make mistakes, but they don't quit."
Conrad Hilton

"Success is a state of mind. If you want success,
start thinking of yourself as a success".
Joyce Brothers

Epilogue

"Success is no accident. It is hard work, perseverance,
learning, studying, sacrifice, and most of all,
love of what you are doing or learning to do."
Pele

In the October / November 2019 issue of Plus Magazine (p. 8), I read an article where a young man was going to perform on the bar.

I quote the article, "The teacher said, "Now, Jim, go on up there and perform on that bar. You can do it!'

"Sir, I can't," the boy whispered. "I'm scared to death."

Then the teacher gave him a simple but profound thought "Throw your heart over that bar and your body will follow."

Think about your uniqueness. When you make up your mind to achieve, then believe that you can. Put your ALL into what you are doing or learning to do and soar.

That will change your life.

"Those who trust in the Lord will renew their strength.
They will soar high on wings like eagles.
They will run and not grow weary.
They will walk and not faint."
Isaiah 40:31

www.ingramcontent.com/pod-product-compliance
Lightning Source LLC
Chambersburg PA
CBHW051601120626
46551CB00013B/1620